THREE FLOWERS
of
Willie J. Etsunen London

By

Angelina McCleod

First published by AuthorHouse 05/03/04

ISBN: 1-4184-6200-4 (e-book)
ISBN: 1-4184-4627-0 (Paperback)
ISBN: 1-4184-4626-2 (Dust Jacket)

Library of Congress Control Number: 2003099503

This book is printed on acid free paper.

Printed in the United States of America
Bloomington, IN

TABLE OF CONTENT

ACKNOWLEDGEMENT

All…

Thank you,

Thank you,

Thank you.

DEDICATION

To Amanada, Kristy, Tina, Annie May
Angie, Annie Lee, Gayle, Margie,
Alice B., Carrie, Tess M., Josephine M.,
Darlene M., Dale K., Eleanor, Sheryl B,
Bonni N., and you.

PREFACE

In 1998, the New Paltz, New York, Friends(Quakers) Meeting House members Kathleen Maloney and Lilla Wilson presented an art show of prisoners' artwork to benefit Family's Domestic Shelter.

Violence At least 50 percent of each sale went to benefit Family's Domestic Violence Shelter.

Most of the poems contained in THREE FLOWERS were written as encouragement to recipients of domestic violence and abuse. The women attending the art showing at the private opening reception and Amanada, Kristy, Annie May, Tina, Angie, Annie Lee, Alice B., Josephine M., Darline M., Margie, and Gayle J., Sheryl B., Bonni N., Sharon A. and you encouraged THREE FLOWERS.

Willie J. Etsunen London

FIRST

I

THE POEM

The Poem

Is the hand in motion

To the zipper of your soul

Onward opening

The bones of your soul

Setting marrow free.

Angelina McCleod

WOMEN ARE CONQUERORS

Women are conquerors

When they conquer

The intoxication of

Silence.

IN HAIKU

Your own silence

Is the reason why

Things stay the same.

Angelina McCleod

FOR REAL

Some of the best works

Have no cover.

CHAINED LOVE

Packed mules

Weighted down

Unloaded set free.

Angelina McCleod

WORD TO WORD

There are not levels of love
like dusk to darkness to dawn
A word to attach pleasurable
While holding hate in another hand
Palm to palm, assuming to combine both
But mean, angry blows scatter
Lamb's sacrificial blood on sheets—
Wife, a woman, a woman torn, battered
And beaten.

COLD HEARTED HATRED

The heart of battering is cold;

The expression and liberties

Of battering is suffering;

The battered is coldly examined;

The reality of battering is hatred.

Angelina McCleod

NOT THE FIRST TIME IGNORED

Screams echo through the night, Ill omens dressed in negligee, Beaten
and battered wife

And stereo-phonographs' volume turned

Louder and louder

But this night beaten and repeatedly

Stabbed, Butcher's knife kissed her jugular

And weeks later the husband's charged

And his neighbors say:

"It's a shame this could have happened To such nice people."

MINDFULNESS

Roaches

Marching through cabinets

Surprised by my shoe.

PRISON EVERYWHERE

For a man to love a man

He is considered queer;

For man to have tenderness

For another man

He is viewed as gay;

For man to live without affection

He lives as he lives today and

Dies as he dies today.

LIVING

Cigarettes are like people

Burn down leaving ashes

Or sweet smelling flowers.

TWO FATHERS

The father of the son:
"Why don't fathers teach their daughters
To be obedient?"

The father of the daughter:
"When the boy's father shows his son
To respect his mother and father's wife."

SCREAM ROOM

I crawl into my scream room

Shriek, squeal, screams, lamenting

Wails of battered defeat

Echo from wall to wall—

At each release from me—anger, hatred, pain

Pain, animosity, resentment, failure, beating

Taken out on me, placed upon me

Echo from wall to wall out of me—

Moments that are freeing, relieving,

renewing And I open the window releasing it

Into the sunlight to be destroyed

Until I retrieve it, giving it life again

And crawling back into my scream room.

CHILD'S LOVE

You are stubborn

Just like your father

Good for notin'

Negatives always applied to Daddy

Attitude shift

To blame the other person

Of the child's love.

S E C O N D

II

UNTOLLED ABUSE

Mother talking negatively
Hatefully to her children
About their father.

Angelina McCleod

IS IT

Better to feel nothing
For another human being
Than to hate, resent, envy
Or desire to destroy him or her?

LIFE'S FARMER

A farmer had a prize rooster

He mated with a prize hen

He was sure of having prize offsprings

But out of the eggshells

Came ducks.

Angelina McCleod

THE MOST BEAUTIFUL FIGURE

Of a woman
Starts from within.

WISDOM BY NATURE

Leaves of autumn

Apple blossoms of spring

An elder's hand.

Angelina McCleod

WOMAN

Summer's full moon

Apple blossoms

I bow.

CONFINEMENT

To be denied all around

To be left searching sacred

Life, wisdom and understanding

To starve for a loving

Tender hand

And a non-destructive thought.

Angelina McCleod

INTO HER EYES

Look into her eyes, batterer,

Implanted fear,

Failure, cowardice

Blow by blow;

Her response is not in love

Respect or honor,

But less of a woman

Reflecting less of a man.

SELF DECEPTION

Men are conquerors
When they conquer
The intoxication of
Male dominance.

LOVE

Love
Is the ultimate
Freedom.

BELIEVE

You are the power

And glory,

The light and victorious,

Beautiful and leader Love.

Angelina McCleod

IS IT JUST IS

When the lights go out
I greet a strange and wonderful
Friend
Then break it with a lit match
For I am afraid
Of what I do not understand.

REACHING INTO ONE'S MIND

Reaching into one's mind

For the universe

Is like reaching for a lit match

In the dark.

Angelina McCleod

KNIGHTLINE

There is a prison in each of us
Many more spend time in self pity
While the world and their own life
A speck in time
Snaps birth to death.

There is a prison in each of us
The battered and abused
The kicks and fists and flaming words
From a home warden and prison guard—who
Attempt loving and caring moments
When rage gives little mercy.
Rage don't care, the prison is me.

DRIED TEARS

Help me to understand my life
Perpetual grief and strife
Is what I embrace
In a windowless room.

I am tired…Drying tears.
Help me to understand my life
Has beauty, ugliness, suffering and pain—
All held in my hand.

Today I decide to take control of my life;
Out of all the pain, suffering, ugliness and beauty
Tears race to puddle paths before me
And I cry lamenting hopelessly without hope
That is what I chose and embraced
And now reject…for my life is me.

T H I R D

III

STRANGER STILL

Never discard your individuality
Your self-identity to embrace another
By submerging in a marriage
It'll be most difficult to regain
When he marriage ends
And, you'll be most lost.

Embracing another's identity
With its concepts, perceptions and services
By a marriage name change
Embracing a stranger.

Angelina McCleod

ONE'S MIND

One's mind is like a tunnel

With no bottom

no sides

no top

no end

And no tunnel.

AND RACISM

Maggots

Like hate

Eat before you realize

It shows.

Angelina McCleod

THAT'S RIDICULOUS

If I could

I would correct all the wrong

I have done in my life.

WORN OLD BOOTS

NATURE'S SCENT
CITY REFUGE DUMP.

Angelina McCleod

WORN OLD BOOTS

Tall oak trees many years old
Cut down with age.

A WORLD WITHOUT SOFTNESS

Cell walls

One kiss blown to the wind

Memories sink behind closed doors

When seen once more

Summoned in time to bloom again

Passing years a chime

Fading away a tear's thought

Grown in the weed of memory.

MY LIFE IS A TREE

Another leaf
Turning before rain.

YOUR LIFE

The tree
The limb
The fruit.

Angelina McCleod

APPLE PICKING

Trees weighted down
Limbs set free.

VERIFICATION

O' spirit to flesh

Hear my soul:

"I love you."

Validation.

Angelina McCleod

NINE FLOWERS

IN A VASE
TRYING TO REFLECT.

A SMILE

Refreshing water

Filling empty cups

With no bottom.

F O U R T H

IV

TODAY'S LOVE

Women with strangers
Held tightly
In their arms.

Angelina McCleod

IN PRISON

Death of a love
Grieving is hard
Softer than prison.

IT WILL

Batterer's song:

"I'm so sorry; I love you;

It won't happen again."

Angelina McCleod

HEAVEN AND HELL

Priest telling battered wife

God requires her to go

Back home and work

On her marriage.

RETURN TO SENDER

Afraid of being lonely,

A failure,

Fractured spirit

Depleted self-confidence,

Broken heart,

Mind games, but no cure

Returning to batterer's arms.

Angelina McCleod

AFTER THE WEDDING BELLS

The rain (tears) washed mascara

Streaks my face

Leaving Christ Crosses, prison bars

That imprison my face and hope

And unreal expectations realized.

BATTERED WIFE'S HANDCUFFS

He needs me;

It's my fault;

He will change;

The children need him;

He loves me.

Angelina McCleod

DEEP BLANK STARE

A woman's thoughts
Trance determining
To stay or go.

CAN'T HIDE THE CRY

Woman repressing her

Cries and pleas

For mercy of battering

Fist and feet

So children won't hear

And cry.

BATTERER TO BATTERED

"Thank you
For allowing me."

IGNORANCE

Raped for fifteen minutes

Media say:

"She was not hurt."

Angelina McCleod

STRUGGLE

Cleansing the mind
Of years of abuse
Accepted abuse.

LABORIOUS STRUGGLE

A battered woman

Accepting

She is not responsible.

Angelina McCleod

INTERNALIZED VICTIM

A victim never overcomes

But relives,

Dies,

Relives,

Dies,

Relives.

DIFFICULTY

Fueling the soul's spark

That say:

"I love you."

Angelina McCleod

NOT SO SIMPLE

Never get married

For the wrong reasons

Cause you

Will have the right reasons

For divorce.

FIFTH

V

YOUR SAGE

Most vulnerable woman
an open hand
Most vulnerable woman
a closed hand
Most vulnerable woman
not knowing when to
open or close.

Angelina McCleod

THE POWER OF WOMAN

The power of woman
Begins within.

Women give away
Their power to men
Freely,
Willingly.

Angelina McCleod

ONE

The power you give away

Is the power

Used to control you.

TWO

It is not how tall or how large you are
But it is how much you want what you want
And how much you are willing to work
To get it.

THREE

The difficulty with giving up

On yourself

Is not knowing

When to start again.

FOUR

The will to win must be greater

Than the desire to lose

By doubting yourself.

Angelina McCleod

IM OR OR

The difference
Between victim
And victor
is or.

SHOULD HE KNOW

I never told him

I just wanted a hug A kiss,

To hold hands,

To be needed and appreciated,

To be wanted,

To be me.

Angelina McCleod

LOVE NEVER CHANGED

Out of the house of bondage

Love never changed,

Only view of him or her.

ENLIGHTENMENT

Inner clarity

Liberates

Liberates, and

Liberates inner clarity.

Angelina McCleod

UNTITLED

It is difficult to see your image

And know the difference

Between the real and illusory.

KNOW NO

When a woman says, "No!"
That should be the end
Of the play…drama.
It's too late to talk about it,
Unless acting to control and
Dominate.

Angelina McCleod

MY DAUGHTER SAID

He won't do anything
He's just following me
Showing up wherever I go
Watching me, hawking me
Stalking me, never let me be.
He won't do nothin' Nothin'."
Her funeral's today.

S I X T H

VI

TO BATTERER

Why do you hate?
The greater prison
With absolute terror
Is constructed in the mind,
Heart and household.

"I AM A VICTIM"

She repetitiously moaned in her
Spirit, "I am a victim."
Therefore and thereby relinquishing
Power and ability to change, to overcome

And to go forward
But remain self-pitying
Continued re-victimization, delusion,
Dissatisfaction and failure.

AGAINST THE ODDS

Women are overcomers

Staying focused on

"I can,"

"I will."

Angelina McCleod

BATTERED WIFE

Painted-over diamond

Balancing of the vitality

Of the world of the living

With the world of the dead.

SEE THE REIN COMING

A motto of resistance

Is a blind spirit feeding reason

And action that runs through

A victor'smind

Lodging in the heart.

Angelina McCleod

ALIENATION

Time spent in self-pity
Is forgetting everything
Else exists.

DOMESTIC VIOLENCE, ET AL.

Plain human thought would never

Conceive of the depths of evil

As it is manifested today

By silence.

NO EXCUSES

There are no excuses

For domestic violence and abuse,

And keeping silent about it.

FIVE

Woman

Your voice is strong

Conquering

Freeing.

NOW

You can put off hurting
Put off silence.

SIX

When you mingle your soul

With your soul-mate

You mingle defeat.

MY VOW

Woman, I love you,

Know nothing else is true.

I will be with you when others run away;

I will fly, lie, violently cry with you

Whenever you feel the need too;

I will be with you

When you feel joy or sorrow, hurt or alone

Or lonely and when you are born, die, reborn.

I will be with you

When you sit silently alone or in a crowd

Or in your blissful corner space;

I will be with you

When you feel lonely,

Walking in the woods,

Forest or on a crowded street.

I will hold you, caress you, kiss your feet

Sitting on a park bench or movie seat.

I will encourage you, cue you before

Danger and plead you won't ignore me.

I will caress your body and mind each

Moment and be your lover as you unwind

I will carry your every burden, large or

Small, and encourage you to stay or go when

Conditions, battered addiction, cloud logic

I will be with you

Whether you stand, crawl, or fall—

I will lift you, heed my urge.

I will teach you to hear what's not spoken

And to discern death or life-giving words

And to overcome what appears unconquerable.

I will be your power, your courage,

Your energy, your woman source.

I am your still, quiet voice

Your inner-being, your Spirit

Your Soul.

EIGHT

Greatest happiness,

Proof of being special

Did not come giving child-birth

But rather when standing

Before a full-length mirror And saying:

"I love you."

NINE

Woman, you are not a failure;

There is no such thing as failure

In a woman;

There are setbacks

And difficulties

And non-mindfulness.

TEN

Peace never comes
With abuse.

YOUR PAGE

IN THE UNITED STATES

If you are a recipient of domestic violence and abuse, you. may call the police. If a police officer has responded, you may request assistance in providing for your safety and for that of your children. You may ask for assistance to obtain an order of protection. You may request the officer assist you in obtaining your essential personal effects, and in locating and taking you and your children to a safe place within the officer's jurisdictions that is, a domestic violence shelter and program, a family member's or friend's residence or other place of safety. You may ask the officer to take you or make arrangements to take you and your children to a place of safety in the county where the incident occurred. If you or your children need medical treatment, you have the right to request the officer assist you in obtaining such treatment. You may request a copy of any incident report, at no cost, from the law enforcement agency that you or the officer made regarding the incident.

You may ask the State Prosecutor, the officer or a law enforcement officer to file a criminal complaint against your abuser. You have the right to file a petition in family court when a family offense has been committed against you. You have the right to have your petition and request for an order of protection filed on the same day you appear in court, and such request must be heard that same day or the next day court is in session. Which ever court is in session, family or criminal court, you may obtain an order of protection which could include an order for the respondent or the defendant to stay away from you and your children. The family court may also order the payment of temporary child support and award temporary custody of your children. You have the right to seek legal counsel of your choosing, or if you cannot afford an attorney, one must be appointed to represent you without cost to you. It is against the law to knowingly file a criminal complaint or family petition that contains false allegations.

INFORMATION

Crisis Intervention

Information for assistance and referrals:

Translate 139 languages, 24 hour, 7 days a week. 1-800-799 SAFE (7233) a National Hotline, and 1-800-787-3224 TDD for the hearing impaired.

Rape, Abuse, and Incest National Network (RAIN)

1-800-656 HOPE

     //feminist.dom/rainn.htm rainn.org

A Confidential Hotline and Hotlines, Shelters.

Missing and Exploited Children: 1-8oo-THE LOST

(1-800-843-5678) www.missingkids.com

(inside back cover page)

THREE FLOWERS

The writings of Willie J. Etsunen London

84-A-0483

Eastern New York Correctional Facility

Box 338

Napanoch, New York 12458-0338

ABOUT THE AUTHOR

Willie J. Etsunen London, B.S., Canisius College of Buffalo, New York. He is an educator and published writer, he is co-editor of "Prison Masculinities," Temple University Press and "A Special Issue: Men in Prison" by Men's Studies Review, 1992, University of California at Berkley. He has completed "Tunes of a Prison Horn" a collection of poems and presently writing a novel and collection of short stories. He has been in prison for over twenty-plus years, counseled rapers, domestic violence and abusers in prison and dialogued with women and men recipients of violence and abuse.

Angelina McCleod, B.S., University of California at Davis, Letters & Science. She has personally experienced and viewed acts of domestic violence and abuse.

www.ingramcontent.com/pod-product-compliance
Lightning Source LLC
Chambersburg PA
CBHW051444280526
45785CB00003B/1414